HOW TO ANALYZE PEOPLE

THE ULTIMATE GUIDE TO SPEED READING PEOPLE THROUGH BEHAVIORAL PSYCHOLOGY, ANALYZING BODY LANGUAGE, UNDERSTAND WHAT EVERY PERSON IS SAYING USING EMOTIONAL INTELLIGENCE, DARK.

ROBERT LEARY

How To Analyze People

The ultimate guide to speed reading people through behavioral psychology, analyzing body language, understand what every person is saying using emotional intelligence, dark.

Table of Contents

Introduction

It is a psychologist's job to be able to read a person's body language precisely. You don't have to be a hardcore psychologist with years of education under your belt to be able to read a person's body language. You, too, can interpret verbal and nonverbal cues in order to understand a person's true personality and identity. If you want to see past a person's mask and perceive their real personality, you have to look at more than just what they vocally tell you. You have to be able to look at all of their body language cues, in addition to what they tell you, and then compare the two. You also must be willing to give away any preconceptions or emotional baggage between yourself and that person, which could stop you from seeing them clearly. By removing any sort of bias and by staying objective, you will be able to receive information about that person without distorting it in any way. Whether you're trying to read your boss, coworker, or even a loved one, in order to completely understand a person's body language, you must *completely* surrender all biases. Benefits of being able to do this are insurmountable. By understanding how those around you are feeling, you will be able to adapt your own message and communication style in order to ensure that it is received in the best possible way. Thus, what sort of things should you be paying attention to? What should you be looking out for? What signs can tip you off to what a person is feeling? All of these and more will be covered within this text.

Continue reading if you would like to know how you can properly and easily read a person and how you can control your own body language. Within the first chapter of this text, I will go into detail about how anyone has the ability to read those around them like a book. I will give a detailed explanation of how easy it is to read those around you and how anyone can learn to read people. I will also give the basics of analyzing those around you.

Within the next chapter, I will go into details about how our bodies talk through language. I will explain how every single part of our body communicates how we feel. Through different motions and the tensing of different muscles, our bodies can show a wide variety of emotions. I will also discuss some common gestures and what they mean in different situations. I will also go into detail about very common nonverbal signals that the body gives off and what they mean in different situations. I will go into detail about the common signals given off through a person's torso, hips, chest, shoulders, and more.

Within the third chapter, I will begin to go into the basic rules for analyzing those around you. These will be the building blocks that you will need in order to begin reading those around you.

Within the fourth and next chapter, I will begin to compare verbal vs. nonverbal communication. I will go in-depth into the differences between verbal and nonverbal behavior. I will also analyze many different types of verbal statements that people may make in certain situations. I will also go into detail about how verbal behavior and nonverbal behavior work together to create a whole picture. I will also go into the intricacies of analyzing nonverbal behavior in order to understand those around you better.

Within the fifth chapter, I will go into an in-depth explanation of the anatomy of our brains and how they contribute to the way that we communicate with others. I will go into the widely loved theory of the unconscious mind and how it relates to our unconscious body language. I will also give some background on the limbic brain and how this connects to our unconscious mind.

Within the sixth chapter, I will go in-depth into the intricacies of facial reading. I will explain how the face is the most important method of nonverbal communication upon our bodies. I will explain how the face contains an extreme amount of delicate muscles that allow us to express a wide variety of emotions. I will also explain how we can easily read our facial expressions and learn to understand them better. I will then go into analyzing every expressive part of the face. These parts will include but are not limited to our eyes, our smiles, our expressions, our lips, our foreheads, and many others.

Within the seventh chapter, I will go into detail about the truth and how it relates to relationships. I will explain how you can tell through body language if a person is lying to another individual. I will also explain how you can analyze a relationship through body language. I will also go into detail about how you can easily judge if a person in a romantic relationship truly loves the other individual within that relationship. I will explain how body language serves as a very important form of nonverbal communication in a loving relationship. I will also go into some almond signs that a female is looking to date a male further. Within this section, I will explain how a woman will put off many different nonverbal signs that she's interested in continuing a long-lasting relationship with a man. After this, I will go into detail about many signals indicating that a man is interested in dating someone for the long-term. I will explain the differences between a man looking for a hookup and a man looking to date somebody for quite some time.

As for the eighth chapter, I will go into the different ways that confidence is displayed upon the human body. I will explain how you can fake your own confidence, as well as how you can spot a lack of confidence in *those around you*. From this, you can also learn how to spot a lack of confidence within *yourself* and how you can improve it.

Within the ninth and final chapter, I will go into detail about how you, too, can fake your own body language so that those around you believe that you feel certain emotions—when in reality, you do not. I will also go into detail about how you can calm your face and relax your muscles so that you're harder to read by those that are good at reading body language. I hope that you enjoy the book and that you find usefulness in the tips and tricks that are included in this text.

Chapter One: How Can Anyone Read People?

If you're anything like me, you love a good mystery-detective. Everybody knows the greatest mystery-detective of all time—that is Sherlock Holmes, of course. Sherlock Holmes is most well-known as the master of deductive reasoning and common literary circles. This character is famous for his innate ability to look at a person and know their entire life story. From the breakfast that they had that morning to some type of traumatic event of their childhood, he can guess it from just one look. You may be thinking that this is simply the stuff of fiction—well, for the most part, you are correct. However, you may be surprised at just how powerful understanding one's body language can be.

A recent study at MIT found that the result of negotiations could be positively predicted by only body language approximately eighty-seven percent of the time. You may be thinking, "This is incredible; all of my dreams are coming true! Sherlock Holmes is real!" Well, not so fast. Yes, you can read a lot more about a person through their body language than one might expect—but it is based on a much more different system than people typically think. Most of the common ideas behind the analysis of a person through their body language are based solely on myth and misconceptions. The real research behind reading a person's body language is quite different from what we have been taught as small children through television and movies. Hence, how exactly do you read people the right way? That is one of the many things that you will learn within this text—before you can do that, you have to understand all of the mistakes that you have been making. Now, we will go into much of the mistakes that people make when trying to read others, in addition to some basic ideas behind reading people's body language.

Context

The biggest thing that people forget to include when they're considering reading somebody's body language is context. Context is everything. There is no one standard rule of thumb when reading somebody's body language—it is all dependent upon the environment that you are in with the person you're trying to read. A person crossing their arms doesn't necessarily have any negative connotation if the room is at a low temperature or if they are sitting in a chair without an armrest. What's more important than these so-called "tells" is the consideration of a situation that somebody is in and the way that they are acting in relation to that. The first thing that you need to consider is the environment that a person is in, and you should try to decide if the way that they are acting or moving their body is cohesive with the environment they're in at that moment.

Considering More Than One Sign

In movies and TV shows about gambling and card games, you often hear people talk about someone having a "tell." These might be things like sweating, face twitching, scratching the nose, or anything in between. In these movies and TV shows, people instantly know when someone's lying because they do one of these "tells." While this is perfect for Hollywood films, this is not how anything *actually* goes down! When trying to read somebody's body language, you need to make sure to consider a group of actions that somebody is performing to tell you what they're really thinking. Hardly ever does a person have one physical action that tells something about themselves. To *really* be able to tell what someone is thinking by looking at their body, you have to ask yourself if the majority of the person's behaviors coincide with common behaviors for a certain emotion.

Not Knowing the Person

Every individual has nervous tics that are different from how they act in a normal situation. Every individual has actions or movements that they do just all the time without any kind of reason behind them. Some people are just jumpy for no reason.

When trying to read somebody's body language, it is crucial to consider how they act in normal situations. Obviously, this isn't helpful if you're meeting somebody for the first time—but typically, getting to know the person first is the primary step to reading their body language. What's more important than looking at what somebody's doing is identifying what they are *not* doing. In other words, if a person is normally jumpy and if for some reason, they are suddenly not, this is when you should be asking yourself, "What's going on right now? why is this person acting like this?"

Biases

Biases are things that we cannot escape as humans. They are something deeply embedded within us all. If you already have certain emotions or feelings towards a person, it will affect or change your judgment when trying to read them. In addition, if somebody tends to compliment you or look and act similar to you, you can be swayed by all of these. The biggest basis of all is truly not having a bias. Hence, it is a good first step to go ahead and assume that you're biased in some way.

With all of these basic ideas in mind, anyone can learn how to read those around them. Whether you wanted for social reasons, business reasons, or even just for fun, learning to read people is simply a matter of trusting your instincts and practicing a skill that you can use in your everyday life.

Chapter Two: Our Bodies and the Way They Talk

I'm sure we have all heard the cliché about how our eyes are the windows to our souls. However, in order to properly read another person like they're a book, you have to be able to look at the big picture. In other words, you have to be able to look at more than just their face, their hands, or just their eyes. You have to be able to read every inch of their body and understand whatever different section of their body is trying to communicate to you, whether they know it or not.

Our emotions are probably the easiest thing we can read through the body. This is because emotions are something that is unconsciously felt, and our bodies respond to them in ways that we can't always control or understand. Typically, we don't even notice when our bodies are doing things that may be revealing our innermost emotions. The reason why this is so difficult to notice and understand is that it is happening all the time without pause. Nonverbal bodily behavior is happening on and around our bodies more frequently than we realize. In addition to this, the interpretation and understanding of these bodily actions, collectively known as our body language, is also occurring simultaneously. By simply glancing at the way that somebody is standing, we can instantly know how they're feeling or how they may feel about us without even realizing that we have made that judgment. This is an incredibly powerful skill to have and is one that humans that have been trying to perfect and use to their advantage for centuries. Understanding the intricacies of body language is a massive foot that takes a lot of studying and hard work. However, we aren't beginning at square one. As people, we have an automatic and internal understanding of universal emotions. A few examples of these are how we smile we smile when we are happy, how we frown when are sad or angry, or how we nod our heads when answering yes. With a few exceptions, the majority of these movements and expressions are commonly understood around the world. This makes our job of understanding body language that much easier but simultaneously harder. Because of how simple and easy to understand these expressions are, following the same train of thought, they are also very easy for people to fake. This makes our job a little bit harder because, in addition to simply knowing the tell-tale signs of certain emotions, we also have to know how to tell if someone is trying to fake them.

Within the next section, this text will begin to discuss some very basic common gestures that people use and what they may mean in different contexts. It is important to keep in mind that the following gestures and interpretations are very basic and surface-level. If you are looking to read into somebody's emotions properly, you should do a lot more than just knowing these basic gestures and their meanings. We will go into more detail about those later in this chapter.

Positive Bodily Gestures

Many common bodily gestures can be broken up at a very basic level into positive body language and negative body language. The following are some very basic signs of *positive* body language:

- Relaxed or uncrossed limbs

If somebody appears relaxed or that they have all of their limbs uncrossed in front of you, this is typically a sign that they are comfortable in your presence. Please keep in mind, though, that this is very easy to fake. Also, remember that what somebody looks like when they are relaxed is very subjective. Relaxed-looking to somebody may be very different for someone else.

- Open palms

Somebody presenting their palms to you open and face up typically is a sign that they trust you and are comfortable around you. This is most likely connected to the fact that when your palms are exposed, so are your wrists. Moreover, it is a very well-known fact that our wrists have some of the largest and most concentrated arteries within our bodies. Hence, the act of opening our palms and laying our hands out in front of somebody is similar to that of a dog that rolls onto its back to expose their stomach to another. It is a sign of trust and submission.

- Leaning forward

The act of someone leaning forward into you can show many things. It can show that somebody is listening very intently to what you are saying to them. It can also show that someone is very, very interested in your ideas or that they hold your beliefs to a very high value. They may view you as someone of high stature that's worth listening to. It can also be a sign that somebody likes you either in a platonic or romantic way. Somebody leaning onto you or towards you shows that they want to get closer to you.

- The speed of speech

This type of body language is a little bit different from those that we have discussed previously. Despite the fact that this body language is also a form of local language, it also falls under the umbrella of body language gestures. The speed of somebody speech can tell a lot about how they actually feel about what they're saying. If somebody is speaking very quickly, it may show that the person speaking is feeling unsure or disorganized. They might know what they want to say or the basis behind what they're saying, but in reality, they could end up talking very fast—maybe because they want to get rid of the words or because they don't feel comfortable when speaking. Alternatively, this could show that they're excited about a subject matter and cannot control themselves when speaking about it. This is also a sign of nervousness and very common in people that are opposed to public speaking or have difficulty doing so. Speaking at an average pace is usually a sign of a very good and well-rounded public speaker. Similar to speaking in a quick tone, slowly speaking can also be a sign that somebody is unsure of what they're trying to say. Unlike speaking quickly, somebody speaking very slowly is often trying to make up what they say on the spot. This may be a sign that they did not prepare properly beforehand, and this tends to give the impression of low intelligence, regardless if this is true or not.

- Pupil size

This is a type of body language that gets passed around very often on the Internet and is often misunderstood. People often believe or say that having enlarged pupils is a sign of love or having a crush on an individual. While these two things are related, they are not necessarily indicators of one another. This is also a troublesome body language to look out for because it is very easy to fake or to stop from happening. If somebody is aware that their body is doing this and doesn't want the other person to know, changing their pupil size is as simple as staring directly into a bright light. If a person is unaware that this is happening, this can be a very strong indicator of what somebody's feeling. Enlargement of the pupils can also show a great deal of interest—if somebody's talking about a topic that they are very passionate about, they may have signs of enlarged pupils due to the intensity of the conversation.

Negative Bodily Gestures

Meanwhile, the following are some very basic examples of *negative* body language:

- Leaning away

The exact opposite of somebody leaning forward has, as you would expect, the opposite meaning of somebody leaning into you. If somebody is leaning away from you, it can have many different interpretations. Depending on what the conversation is about, someone could be leaning away from you because you said something that they felt to be quite shocking. You may have said something that they highly disagree with or something against some of their core beliefs. If you have not been having a controversial conversation, it is possible that a person leaning away from you just doesn't like you or doesn't want to be in your presence.

- Crossed limbs

The action of somebody crossing their limbs can have various meanings. Depending on the situation, at a very surface-level, somebody crossing their arms could be taking a defensive position. They could also be taking a position of discomfort. They could be trying to hide more of their body, or they could also be trying to make their body seem smaller. This can often be a sign of discomfort or self-consciousness in a moment. Somebody may have recently said something that makes them feel uncomfortable, which then prompted them to feel the need to hide their body. This position can also show signs of anger or a disgruntled feeling at a statement somebody has made.

- Tight shoulders

If somebody's shoulders appear to be very tight, this is often a sign that they're under some kind of stress. They might have a lot of things on their plate, or they might be uncomfortable talking to a certain person. They might feel as though they're walking on eggshells or as though they need to be very careful about what they say. An individual with shoulders that are very unrelaxed and push up high to their chin might be nervous or feel unwelcome in a situation.

- Feet turned away

This position may seem somewhat random or unconnected compared to all of the others. However, watch out for this sign because it appears more often than one may believe. If somebody who's standing in front of you points their feet away from or towards an exit, they may be indicating that they want to end a conversation. Alternatively, they may be indicating that they are late for something or that they need to leave as soon as possible or simply that they don't want to talk to you anymore.

- Leaning on two hands or head resting on one hand

If an individual is sitting at a desk and has their chin on their hand, this can mean one of two things. This is an indicator that somebody is either incredibly bored or thinking very intensely. Typically, you can tell the difference between these two by looking at the rest of the person's body. Are they slouching? Are their eyes half-closed, or are they fully open? Have they yawned recently? Depending on the answers to these questions, you may be able to determine whether a person is resting their head in their hand because they're too bored to hold it up or if they're simply thinking of something very intensely and can't be bothered to hold their head up themselves.

As we have discussed previously, reading body language is about a lot more than most of these common gestures alone. You have to look at the bigger picture and take into account the interpretations of every inch of that person's body. In the next section of this book, we will be going into detail about the nonverbal aspects of the body and what they mean. You will go through every well-known appendage and part of the human body—from torso, hips, chest, feet, and more.

Torso

Many individuals attempting to learn how to read body language make the mistake of ignoring the torso as a signal-giving part of the body. This is a huge and detrimental mistake to make. Torso makes up the vast majority of the body and, as such, is responsible for approximately seventy percent of the signals that we give off. Leaving out the torso in our consideration of body language leaves out a huge chunk of the body to read. If somebody does this, then they will not receive the big picture when trying to read a person. When looking at the body language of the torso, we have to break the torso up into multiple languages in order to fully understand it.

- Neck

The neck, used to support the head, is a very important part of our body to read.

  - Hiding - the act of hiding one's neck is an instinctive one that happens when someone feels threatened. This comes from a biological understanding of a predator attempting to attack possibly the most vulnerable parts of the body.

People have an instinct to try and hide their body part that they feel threatened. Because of the way that humans have evolved and adapted to everyday life, they could find themselves hiding their necks if they feel threatened at things that have no real physical consequences for them. We can then find ourselves hiding our necks if we feel threatened for our jobs or our respective socio-economic situations. If a person is feeling embarrassed, they may also find themselves reaching out to touch their neck or swallowing more than average.

- Touching - the act of touching the front of the neck or the location of the windpipe may show concern about what an individual is saying to them. They instinctively may reach up to touch their windpipe because that is where the concerning words are going to come from. It is also important to note that the back of the neck contains some very strong and large muscles. If a person is rubbing or massaging those muscles, this may be a sign of tension or stress.

- Shoulders

If a person's arms are folded in front of them, then their shoulders will naturally be curved forward without them needing to do it themselves. If a person's arms are not crossed but instead are hanging down by their side, there can be a wide range of emotions and feelings.

- Raised - if the shoulders are seen to be in a raised position, then the person whose shoulders are raised are having to pull the entire weight of their arms all the way up. This takes a great amount of effort compared to other body language symbols. Because this, this is a very conscious symbol of body language and is often something that somebody's doing intentionally. When this is added with arms folded tight over the body or holding the body, it can be a sign of colds or of great levels of tension.
- Curved forward - in case that the shoulders are curved forward, they're attempting to lower the width of the body, which is often used as a defensive posture or a subconscious attempt to not be seen. If a person is feeling embarrassed or threatened in any way, then they may have this position.
- Pushed back - the act of pushing one's shoulders backward forces the chest out and shows the torso to potential attacked. Because of this, this posture is often used when a person is trying to appear confident and maybe trying to

demonstrate great power.

- Circling - the act of circling one's shoulders either forward or backward is usually done to exercise a stiff or tense shoulder. In most situations, this is simply a sign that a person is feeling very stressed.
- Leaning - when a person is seen to lean against the wall, they have to make contact with the wall and their shoulder. This is usually a sign of relaxation or a symbol that shifting into physical movement would take more effort than simply leaning against the wall. This puts a person in a position that is vulnerable to attack, but it is typically very clear that the said person's okay with that. Oftentimes, this is seen as meaning that an individual doesn't view another individual as a threat or is trying to come off as confident or cocky.
- Turning - the act of turning one's shoulders away from somebody is a sign that they want to end a conversation or do not want to continue talking to you. If they are still talking to you while doing this, they may be trying to send you unconscious signals to end the conversation. If a person is trying towards you, it shows that they are very interested in what you were saying.

- Chest

The chest sends a few body language symbols that are very important.

- Thrusting outwards – oftentimes, thrusting draws attention to the person doing it. Women, in particular, have a tendency to do this, as they are programmed to know that men are aroused by the sight of breasts. When a female is pushing forward their breasts, they may be unconsciously or even consciously inviting intimate relations. It is important to note that high heels enhance this factor, as they promote curvature in the spine, which pushes the chest and buttocks outwards. Men also have a tendency to push out their chests in the temp to attract a mate. This is often in the hopes of displaying large or strong pectorals. The big difference between men and women is that men can also do this to other men, in addition to women, typically in an attempt to intimidate the men around them.
- Profile - when a person is standing sideways, or at a forty-five-degree angle, then the effect of the previously discussed pushed-out chest is even more exaggerated. This may be used by women to show off the curve of their breasts

or by men to show off the size of their pectorals.
- Withdrawn - the chest contains some of the most important and most vulnerable organs in the human body. Well, somewhat protected by the ribs, they are still very vulnerable to attack. When the chest is being pulled into itself, it may serve as a sign that a person is trying to appear unthreatening are trying their best to disappear to prevent themselves from being attacked.
- Breathing - when a person is viewed to be breathing very deeply, then the chest tends to move up and down with much more extreme than normal. A deep breath is a sign that somebody may be taking in a lot of oxygen and readying for action. This may be a sign of extreme anger or very intense feeling such as love.

- **Hips**

The hips are at the base of the torso and make up the pelvis and buttocks. They are a crucial form of body language.

- Thrusting out - the hips on both genders contain the primary sexual organs, and as a result, dressing them forward is a sign of provocation and suggestion. This is further exaggerated if the legs are spread—exposing the genitals further and inviting action. Pushing our hips forward is difficult to do without losing our balance, so this can be done by leaning against something like a well that may support the upper body.
- Holding back - the action of holding back the hips—as I'm sure you can guess—is the opposite of pushing them outwards. It hides genitals and seeks to protect them or avoid having them noticed. This may be a sign that somebody is uninterested in you or has no attraction to you whatsoever.
- Pushing to the side - the action of pushing your hips to the side makes it necessary for the entirety of your body to compensate for the rearrangement of the spinal curve. This is typically seen as a relaxed position, as the body is able to drop its center of gravity. A lesser-known meaning of disposition is the hips may be pointing towards a person that they are interested in or may actually be wanting to talk to. If the hips are pointing towards the door, it can mean that the person wants to leave the conversation or the area.
- Touching — Some of the things that may be used as a signal of power or dominance include placing someone's hands on their hips, pushing the elbow

sideways, and making the body look larger. On the flip side of this, stroking of one's hips may be a sign of flirtation in a romantic setting, especially if accompanied by the swaying of hips and prolonged eye contact.

- Hands

Our hands contain up to twenty-seven bones and are the most used part of our bodies. Our hands are very important to everyday function and thus give away a lot in terms of body language.

- Cupping - the action of cupping our hands together creates a form that can serve as a container or bowl. When one's hands come together, this can be a symbol of delicacy or a sign that someone is holding a fragile idea. This can also be used as a sign of giving. The action of holding your hands out to someone in a cup fashion is a sign of giving or showing to another person.
- Greetings - hands are very often used as a form of greeting. The most common type of this is the act of shaking one's hands. This is a type of great team that transcends across many cultures and religions. The act of opening one's palm for another on a subconscious level is to find out if the other person is not carrying a weapon or something meant to harm. This is why the act of opening our palms is used in various greetings such as salutes or waves. Going back to handshakes, there are various ways that you can show certain emotions through them. If an individual places their hands on top of yours during a handshake and holds it longer than you would expect, this can be a sign of asserting dominance. On the opposite end, a handshake with a floppy or loose grip is a sign of submission.
- Rubbing - if a person tends to rub their hands together, it can mean a variety of things. On the surface level, it could mean that the person is simply feeling cold. It could also mean that an individual is feeling happy or excited about something that has transpired. If somebody appears to be rubbing their hands together subtly and slowly, then they may be thinking about a benefit they may gain at the expense of another person.
- Hiding - the act of hiding one's hands—behind the back, in their pockets, under the table, or sitting on top of them—indicates many different communicative meetings. Most often, this is a sign that an individual has a desire not to cooperate with or to listen to the person speaking any longer. It usually is a sign

that they do not agree with something that the speaker has said or that they don't want to talk to them any longer. This may be done deliberately, or a person who has recently lied may hide their hands subconsciously due to the fear of their hands giving them away.

- ○ Trembling - trembling of the hands can mean many different things, and not all of them are necessarily negative. The trembling of one's hands may be a sign that that individual is very frightened, or it could also be a sign that that individual is very excited. Connected to this, an unexpected action like dropping something that somebody is holding can be a sign that their motor skills are somewhat malfunctioning for a particular reason. Whether this reason is that they're nervous, excited, or feeling any kind of extreme emotion will depend on a wide range of factors.

- • Legs

When a person is consciously trying to control their body language, they often focus much too hard on their upper body alone. For this reason, the legs can often tell us a deeper story about what a person is feeling as compared to the upper body.

- ○ Open — if a person originally standing in a stationary position have their legs spread apart, they're providing for themselves a stable base so as to support their upper body and keep their balance. If a person's legs are slightly wider than the width of their shoulders, then this can be a sign that the said individual is feeling grounded and confident that day. In addition, a wider stance can make the body appear larger and is thus a signal of power and dominance.
- ○ Closed - when an individual is standing with their legs being apart less than their shoulders' distance from each another, then this may be displaying a sign of anxiety, as it makes them appear smaller and gives more protection to their genitalia.
- ○ Pointing - an individual's legs can have a tendency to point in the direction of where they wish they could go without them realizing it. If a person's legs are pointing towards a person talking, that means that they are feeling very attentive and are very interested in the conversation that they are in. On the flip side, however, an individual who is pointing their legs opposite the direction of a person they're talking to means that they may want to leave the conversation or

that they want to be elsewhere.

Chapter Three: The Basics

In today's modern world of politics and business, many people now understand that everything has become about appearance and body language over the pure merit of a person. Because of this, the vast majority of high-profile politicians now have their own personal body language consultants that help them come across as being honest, caring, and responsible individuals. Since the 1960s, the evolution of our body language has been actively studied, and the public was brought into the world of our body language through a book titled *Body Language*, which was published in 1978. Despite this, the majority of individuals believe that speech is our main form of communication today. Well, speech is very important in getting across what we believe in to those around us.

Evolutionarily speech has only been with the human race for a very short amount of time. Prior to widespread modern language, you could understand what people meant or felt towards you through only their body language. We are still capable of this today, but it becomes a little bit more difficult because of the weight we put on spoken word. With a few simple tips and tricks, you can begin the basics of reading someone's body language like it is a second language.

The first thing that we are going to discuss is the necessity of being able to understand a person's emotional condition while listening to what they are saying to you and taking that into context with the circumstances under which they are saying it. In simpler terms, you have to understand the *context*. You have to be able to look at every piece of the puzzle—rather than just the corner piece and trying to understand what the picture is. Hence, while you should be listening to what a person is vocally telling you, it is also vital for you to mentally thinking about what that person's emotional condition at that moment is and then compare it to the physical environment around them. If a person is smiling and if their cheeks are bright red, while the room just so happens to be hot at that very moment, that person might not necessarily be embarrassed. They might simply feel hot.

It is interesting to note the connection between a person's gender and their ability to perceive nonverbal communication. There's lots of talk in modern conversations about a "mother's intuition." This is not an old wives' tale. Women have been proven in qualitative scientific studies to be more perceptive at understanding body language than men are. A study done at Harvard University showed that when a random sample of men and women were given the same film with no audio, the women were eighty-seven percent more likely to guess what the circumstances of the situation were, whereas men only guessed correctly forty-two percent of the time. It is believed that women's perceptiveness of body language is superior to men because, for the first few years of raising a child, a mother has to rely almost entirely on nonverbal communication to understand the child's needs and wants. This is supported by the fact that women with children guessed the situation correctly almost every single time. This is also often used to explain why women tend to be better negotiators than men.

Much of basic common body language is the same all over the world despite religion and racial differences. Some examples of this are smiling when you're happy or scowling when you are sad or angry. The nodding of the head is almost completely universally used to indicate an affirmation of sorts. It is believed that this form of affirmation is a genetic predisposition because individuals who were born blind still use this form of body language even though they never learned to use it visually.

This then brings me to an interesting point about body language and whether it is a learned action or genetic action. This is a debate that is ongoing and is still being researched even up to this day. Some forms of body language can be traced back to animal ancestry and are believed to be purely genetic. This is the action of sneering at another person in anger or irritation. An animal's a similar action to this is done when preparing for an attack.

There are three basic rules for an accurate reading of somebody's body language. You must keep these three rules in mind when attempting to analyze any person for their body language.

1. Reading Clusters of Gestures Rather Than an Individual

You should never try to analyze or interpret a single solitary gesture separately from all of the others. You have to look at the entire picture. This means that you have to look at every action of the person's body and compare it to the rest of them. It is easy to remember this rule when you think of body language as just that: a language. As with any vocally spoken language, body language has its own "words," "sentences," and "punctuation." Attempting to understand somebody's body language through one specific gesture is like attempting to understand an entire paragraph from just a single word. You have to read each individual gesture as its own word and put them together to create sentences so that you can understand the language that someone's body is giving off. A common rule of thumb for this is the idea that someone needs at least three words to be able to create a proper sentence. As for body language, this means that you have to be able to compare at least three gestures that a person is giving off before you can begin to understand their innermost feelings and thoughts.

2. Searching for Consistency

This is especially important when trying to decide if somebody may be lying to you or not. Consistency is key in being able to tell if somebody is telling the truth. You have to consider the words that are coming out of their mouth in relation to what their body language is showing you. If an individual's words and body language are in conflict in a given moment, it is often best to ignore what is being said and focus instead on body language exclusively. Inconsistency between body language and vocal words is a strong sign of lying.

3. Context, Context, Context

Context is incredibly important when attempting to read a person's body language. You have to take into account an individual's environment, in addition to the signals that their body is giving off. There are lots of body symbols that have no meaning whatsoever when an individual is in certain situations. For instance, a person with arms and legs crossed tightly together on a cold winter's day is not necessarily a sign of feeling defensive—they are most likely just cold.

Chapter Four: Verbal vs. Nonverbal

Language is incredible. As humans, we have an incredibly heightened ability to communicate with one another. This level of communication is a part of the reason that we have been able to advance so far in our evolution. The advancement of our communication results in advancement in our society. Within this chapter, we will discuss the ways that our communication is more advanced and the intricacies behind verbal and nonverbal behavior. More importantly, we will define nonverbal and verbal behavior and also give two differences between the two and learn how to analyze the statements that other individuals make verbally. More specifically, we will learn how to analyze these verbal statements using nonverbal language. We will also go into the intricacies of analyzing the nonverbal behavior of those around us.

Defining Nonverbal Behavior

Nonverbal behavior or communication is the subconscious or conscious relaying of ideas or emotions through physical motion or a series of well-known and understood gestures. Messages can be transferred non-verbally through a variety of signals and methods.

The first of these defining signals are methods known as proxemics. Proxemics essentially means the distance between two individuals. The distance between two individuals or proxemics carries a lot of weight in terms of nonverbal communication.

The second method of nonverbal communication is known as kinesics and is simply another word for body language. Kinesics or body language is the transmission of ideas through gestures and often unconscious motions of the body.

Meanwhile, another defining method is known as haptics. Haptics is another word for the act of touching something. In the world of nonverbal behavior, the way that somebody touches something carries a lot of weight in communicating their emotions to another individual. A soft touch on the arm can mean a lot of things, which becomes very different in comparison to a firm grasp of one's hand. Not all touches are equal, and every touch—depending on its longevity, intensity, and location on the body—has many different meanings behind it.

Another form of nonverbal communication is our appearance. People use their appearance to communicate their personality in a variety of ways. Most of this is a conscious decision made by the individual, but there are some factors almost entirely caused by our parents that aren't necessarily chosen by us but still say things about ourselves. Most likely, the biggest and most common type of nonverbal communication using our parents is simply judging whether or not somebody cares about their appearance. By just looking at another person, we can instantly tell whether or not they care about how they appear to those around them. This carries a huge amount of weight in the snap judgment that we make about people every single day. The final common form of nonverbal communication is the use of eye contact. Eye contact is extremely important in us as humans. Humans are very focused on an individual's eyes, as that is often one of the first things that a person looks at when they see a new face. Your eyes are often considered the windows to the soul, and this is true in the sense that they can reveal a lot of factors about yourselves. By looking into someone's eyes or measuring the amount of eye contact they give, we can understand a vast amount of information about their personality. Do they have strong eye contact? Do they avoid eye contact? Do they have really intense eye contact? The answers to all of these questions give us different definitions to a person's personality. As humans, we put a lot of weight on to an individual's eye contact as a defining portion of their personality. This is why we must keep eye contact in mind when attempting to understand someone's nonverbal communication.

Defining Verbal Communication

Verbal communication seems quite obvious when spoken out loud. Verbal communication obviously does consist of any form of speech or language that is used to relay ideas or thoughts to another. Verbal communication includes much more than simply speaking to a person. The way that we string together ideas and thoughts with word shows a lot about their personality in the words that we choose in the cadence that we choose to put them together. There are multiple ways that we can express ourselves through verbal communication. The first and most obvious way that we can express ourselves through verbal communication is through speaking to those around us. By stringing together words and sentences, we create cohesive thoughts and ideas that express our feelings to those around us.

In addition to being able to accurately and positively express our emotions and feelings to those around us, the act of speaking is also quite easy to use to persuade or to alter our true meaning. It is much easier to lie to a person verbally than it is to lie to a person with our body language. Because of this, we often find people who lie very easily vocally to a person but whose body language cues do not match their words.

The second form of verbal communication, writing, may come as a surprise to some people reading this text. The act of writing, while not technically verbal, still comprises verbal communication because it uses common vocally spoken language simply in written form. The difficulty in this is that a person reading a text has a much harder time of guessing and understanding the cadence of the person who wrote the text. Because of this, written ideas and emotions can be misconstrued due to the fact that people cannot quite tell the intonation of the author of the text through the words.

Another form of verbal communication is an underlying feeling within our words known as denotation or connotation. The connotation is considered as the feelings or emotions associated with the meanings of certain words or phrases. This is not to be confused with its antonym, denotation, which is the literal or primary meaning of a word, opposite to the emotions or series that the word suggests. In order to convey these important forms of verbal communication, a person has to use our neck form of verbal communication.

The next form of verbal communication that we will be discussing is tone and volume. An individual's tone, when talking to another person, can express a lot about that person's inner thoughts or feelings. The tone is a very difficult form of communication to pin down and explain to people. For some individuals, the tone is very easy to control and change in their language—while for others, it can be very difficult. You cannot describe the tone as based on the inflection that an individual puts on to certain words at certain times. The tone is very interesting because every person is able to understand the meaning behind other people's tones almost in perfect connection with one another, but it is very difficult to explain to others. In connection to this, a person's volume also holds a great deal of significance in their verbal communication. Ever since childhood, we have all learned about the difference between an inside voice and an outside voice. Do volume levels show a lot about our emotions? We can read a lot about how someone feels in a certain situation based on their volume at that time.

It is important always to remember that you have to use *both* verbal and nonverbal forms of communication together in parallel to understand the grand total outcome of a person's ideas and theories. A common misconception amongst individuals is that verbal communication and nonverbal communication are contradictory. This is not the case. Verbal and nonverbal communication must go side-by-side when communicating with those around us. It is the combination of these two complex forms of communication that make the translation of our ideas and theories the most effective. One cannot exist without the other—in most cases. It is often asserted by body language specialists that nonverbal communication can play one of five roles when trying to read another person. These five roles are known as substitution, reinforcement, contradiction, accentuation, and regulation.

Substitution - certain types of nonverbal communication are started as a substitution or placement for verbal communication. Examples of this are nodding your head for yes or shrugging your shoulders for "I don't know."

Reinforcement - nonverbal communication can often be used to reinforce a previously given statement. By reading an individual's body language and judging it consistently, you can almost entirely ascertain whether they are telling the truth or not.

Contradiction - this is the opposite of reinforcement. If a person's body language appears to be contradicting something that they are saying, then by the rule of contradiction, they are almost certainly lying—depending on their environment, of course.

Accentuation - body language often serves as a method of accentuating something that a person says vocally. Examples of this include smiling when someone says that they are happy or shivering when somebody says that they are cold. This can also be used to put a greater level of importance to a statement that somebody has given out. An example of this is creating the quotation mark symbol with your fingers while saying something sarcastically. By adding body language to the statement that you're making, you are reaffirming and showing importance in your statement.

Regulation - an individual's body can also serve to regulate that person's vocal language.

Chapter Five: Your Mind and the Way You Communicate

A lot of an individual's communication is not based solely on what they actively try to put out there. A much larger, much more active chunk of our communication is based on what we don't realize that we are putting out in the world. Our body can reveal our deepest emotions and feelings without us realizing pretty much twenty-four seven. This does not happen randomly, of course. The way that our mind communicates without us realizing it is based on two main theories of thought. These are known as the unconscious mind and the limbic brain. In the following chapter, I will define and give the importance of the unconscious mind and the limbic brain in our communication.

Unconscious Mind

The unconscious mind originates from Freud's Psychoanalytic Theory of Personality. In this theory, Freud defines the unconscious mind as a hidden well of feelings, thoughts, urges, and memories that are separate from our conscious awareness of feelings. The contents of our unconscious mind tend to be unpleasant or depressing. They tend to include feelings of pain, anxiety, or conflict. It is because of these negative feelings and emotions that our unconscious mind stays outside of our conscious awareness. Since on a subconscious level, we do not want to remember or feel those feelings, we then try to ignore them and push them into our unconscious mind.

Despite this attempt at ignoring and hiding these feelings, our unconscious mind still influences our behavior even though we do not know that it is there. Many individuals compare the unconscious mind to that of an iceberg. The part of the iceberg that is above water represents our conscious brain and all of the communication of ideas and feelings that we actively put out into the world. Oppositely, our unconscious mind is represented by every part of the iceberg that is below the water and unseen. Within this iceberg analogy, it is important to remember how large an iceberg below the water truly is. This represents just how deep our unconscious mind goes and just how much tends to be hidden below the surface. The amount of information that is hidden just below the surface within our unconscious mind is so massive like the hidden part of the iceberg in the sense that we have to consider the parts of our body language that connect to our unconscious mind as a huge part of nonverbal communication.

Freud also believed and asserted that our basic instincts and animal urges are contained within the unconscious mind. This includes instincts under actions of life and death as well as sexual instincts. He believed that urges such as these were hidden from or kicked out of our present consciousness because our minds view them as unacceptable, irrational, or uncivilized. Freud suggested that individuals often use a number of different defense mechanisms to stop these hidden urges from rising above the waters into our conscious mind.

Freud also goes on to explain the different ways that the information from the unconscious mind might be brought into conscious awareness. One of the techniques that Freud explained can be used to bring these feelings into awareness is known as free association. Free association is a rather simple and seemingly silly form of psychotherapy. In free association, Freud asked patients to lay back and relax and say to him whatever came to their minds without any sort of filter on it. He wanted them to say anything that they could think of without stopping to think of it is trivial, irrelevant, or embarrassing. Freud then traced the streams of thoughts until he believed that he could uncover the contents of the unconscious mind. He often used this method in order to try to find repressed childhood traumas or hidden desires.

Freud also believes that dream interpretation could be used to understand the unconscious mind further. Many people think of dreams as a route to the unconscious mind and believe that the information from the unconscious mind could appear randomly in dreams but typically in a disguised format. Because of this, he would often ask patients to keep dream journals and would try to go through and interpret these dreams to try and understand their hidden meanings.

Freud also believes that dreams tended to serve as a form of secret fulfillment of long-coddled wishes. He believes that the fact that these unconscious urges were not expressed in real life means that they could be expressed in the individual's dreams.

The Freudian theory of the unconscious mind did not come across as without controversy. A multitude of researchers have criticized the idea of the unconscious mind and firmly dispute that there isn't an unconscious mind at all. Recently, in the field of cognitive psychology, researchers and psychologists have begun to focus on the automatic and instinctive functions that describe things that were previously being attributed to the unconscious mind. The ideas behind this approach believe that there are a series of cognitive functions that happen outside of our conscious awareness.

Meanwhile, they do not entirely support the voice conceptualization of the unconscious mind, but it does offer some evidence that actions that we are not aware of still have an influence on our automatic behaviors. Unlike Freud's psychoanalytic approaches to the unconscious mind, research within the modern field of cognitive psychology is almost exclusively driven by scientific investigation and quantitative data. This idea of the unconscious mind continues to have a great effect on modern psychology and is still used in some modern practices today.

Limbic Brain System

The limbic system within an individual's brain is responsible for a variety of very important brain functions. The biggest responsibility of the limbic system is our instincts for survival and for memory access and storage. The limbic system is made up of many different brain structures—two of the biggest and most important parts of the limbic system are the amygdala and the hippocampus. Amygdala is the deciding structure that chooses where each memory should be placed in the brain, while the hippocampus transports that memory to its final location. It is often believed that the placement is determined by the amount of emotional response that it receives from the person.

The limbic system is also very responsible for hormone levels, body temperature, and motor functions. The different parts of the limbic brain system are the amygdala, cingulate gyrus, the hippocampus, and the hypothalamus. These individual structures are very important parts of a person's brain. The limbic system, as a whole, is located on top of the brainstem and underneath the frontal cortex. The limbic system is often connected to survival-based emotions such as fear, anger, and pleasure. The limbic system is also known to influence both the peripheral nervous system and the endocrine system. The part of the limbic system that is important to this text, in particular, is its connection with memory. Because of the limbic system's perceived importance in the decisions of where memories go and how they are remembered, it is often connected with Freud's ideas of the unconscious mind. Because Freud's ideas of the unconscious mind are based on the theory that certain memories and feelings are hidden far away from our conscious awareness, it is easy to understand how the limbic system can play a huge part in that considering that it is believed to be the deciding factor of where our memories get stored. Now, you may be thinking to yourself, "What does any of this have to do with our body language and understanding the body language of those around us?" The answer lies in the fact that the unconscious mind is very powerful and controls a huge portion of our true feelings and emotions. By reading body language, we can often unlock these feelings of the unconscious mind without even realizing that they are hidden from the person we are reading. This is a very powerful skill, and it is important to understand the basis behind it. The limbic system and the unconscious mind create this basis for the deeper readings of people.

Chapter Six: Intricacies of the Face

Returning to our methods of nonverbal communication and the reading of body language, we come to the intricacies and extreme complications of facial communication. The face is a huge indicator of nonverbal communication within body language. The face tends to tell all. The face is also the most difficult to control when trying to regulate your own body language. Within this chapter, we will discuss the use of the face as a method for nonverbal communication and how we can easily read it on our own. We will also analyze the expressive parts of the face and what they can say in terms of nonverbal communication.

Many parts of the face are the first things consider when we look at a new person. Because of this, a lot can be conveyed within a person's face. This is partially an evolutionary result because we spend so much time looking into the faces of those around us to the point that we have, over time, evolved to be able to convey emotions and expressions on their faces so that those around us may not have to ask to know what we are feeling. There are a few tricks to reading somebody's face beyond a simple basis of whether or not they're angry at you.

The first one is staring into an individual's eyes. When you begin reading a person's face, you will want to start at their eyes. The eyes contain the most expression within a person's face. You can learn an extreme amount of detail about somebody's emotions by paying close attention to their eyes. Later in the chapter, we will go through some common expressions that we can read within the eyes.

The next step is to look at the lips. The muscles in our lips are extremely sensitive and are constantly shifting. A person's lips can move and react to situations without an individual even realizing what they're doing. You can pay attention to a person's lip to figure out how they feel about certain situations or what their next action may be.

The next step may come as a surprise to most individuals. This is to pay attention to the nose. The nose does not change quite as much as the eyes and the lips, but its location on the face makes it a very important part of facial reading. The nose is right in the middle of a person's face. It is because of this that many people tend to glance at a person's nose before they even look at a person's eyes or mouth. Because of this, the nose acts as a grounding or central location to the rest of our face. If an event or a feeling is powerful enough to cause one's nose to move, then you can take that as a sign that whatever happened was groundbreaking enough to shift the very foundation of that person's face.

The next step and part of the face to pay attention to is the eyebrows. Connected to the eyes and often the second most expressive parts of our face, the eyebrows can express a wide variety of emotions. Their ability to move with a great level of dexterity and range puts them at a greater advantage than the rest of our face. In addition, our eyebrows tend to work in connection with our eyes. Hence, by taking in the eyes and the eyebrows as a whole, you can get a complete picture of a person's emotions or feelings about a certain event.

The final step in being able to properly and accurately read a person's face is simply to gain the ability to perceive different emotions upon the face. We will discuss this in further detail later in this chapter as I lay out different emotions that various expressions tend to show.

The Head

The head is often the first thing that a person looks at when they meet a new individual. We spend a lot of our lives looking at a person's head. As a result, the human head is designed to send many signals between individuals. The majority of them tend to be subconscious, which is useful in the context of this book.

- The Face

The human face contains around fifty muscles; the majority of these muscles can be used to send nonverbal signals to those around us. Addition to muscles, the color of the skin and the temperature can also be quite important in understanding nonverbal language from the face.

- Color – colors of the face tell a long and detailed story about what a person is feeling at a given point. If a person's face is very clearly red, they may be showing signals for many different things. In very generic terms, a red face is a sign that someone's face is hot. Whether this is from exercise, emotional arousal, or embarrassment, it is a sign that blood is rushing to the face for one reason or another. It also can be a sign of anger or aggression. Alternatively, the color of the face can also be white. A whiteness of skin may be a sign of coldness and of blood leaving the face. This may be a sign of sickness or fear. A face can also take on a bluish hint when it is very cold or experiencing extreme fear or sickness.
- Dampness – the level of moisture that somebody's face has when you are looking at them can tell a wide variety of feelings. You have to be careful not to look too far into this sign, as the wetness of a person's face can also be caused by simply sweating when it is warm outside. If it is not warm in the area that a person is in and if their face appears to be very damp or covered in a lot of moisture, that person may be feeling fearful, as sweat is often associated with fear. Some scientists theorize that sweating on the face when feeling fear is an evolutionary defense mechanism to make the skin slippery and more difficult for an opponent to get a firm grasp of the face.

Common Facial Signals for Different Emotions

The following are a series of common facial signals that indicate different emotions. It is important to remember that some of these signs are not an instant indicator that a person is feeling the emotion in question. However, a combination of all of these signs may suggest that a person is feeling a certain emotion, depending on the environment surrounding them.

- Common signs of happiness

Some common signs of happiness within the face include but are not limited to:

- The mouth and an open or closed smile sometimes accompanied by laughter or chuckling;
- Possibly some crow's feet type wrinkles at the sides of a person's eyes—this indicates that a smile is honest and real because it is using enough muscles to change the wrinkles and a person's face;
- Eyebrows raised slightly; and
- A person's head tilted back or at a higher level than normal.

- **Common signs of sadness**

Some common signs of sadness within the face and head include but are not limited to:

- A person's eyes are staring downwards at a lower angle than ninety degrees;
- Possibly some dampness or moisture within the eyes;
- Head tilted downwards along with the eyes;
- Lips pinch tightly together or trembling;
- Trembling of the chin; and
- Head tilted to the side.

- **Common signs of anxiety**

Some common signs of anxiety within the face and head include but are not limited to:

- Eyes that are damp or filled with moisture;
- Eyebrows that are pushed together and wrinkled;
- A lower lip trembling or lips pinch together;
- Skin wrinkling or tents; and
- Head tilted downward possibly looking at the ground.

- **Common signals of fear**

A few common signals of fear within the face and head include but are not limited to:

- Eyes wide open with large pupils;

- Eyes closed or pointed downwards;
- Eyebrows raised wrinkling the forehead;
- Open mouth or corners of the mouth turn downwards;
- Chin pulled and tucked into the neck;
- Head tilted downwards possibly staring at the ground; and
- A white-tinted face.

- **Common signals of anger**

Some common signals of anger include but are not limited to:

- Eyes either wide and staring or squinted
- Eyebrows push downwards towards the eyes and possibly forever
- A wrinkled forehead
- Nostrils that are flaring or twitching
- A mouth that is flattened out into a line or teeth that are clearly clenched
- A chine jutting out towards a person
- A face that is red in color

- **Common signals of envy or jealousy**

Some common signals of envy or jealousy within the face and the head include but are not limited to:

- Eyes staring wide with pupils large
- The corners of one's mouth turn downwards
- Crinkling of the nose or sneering at an individual
- Chin that's jutting outwards away from the body

- **Common signs of desire or lust**

Common signals of desire or lust within the face and the head include but are not limited to:

- Eyes open wide with heavily dilated pupils;

- Eyebrows that are raised slightly but softly;
- Lips parted slightly or puckered;
- Stop smiling; and
- Head that is tilted forward or slightly tilted to the side at an angle.

- **Common signs of interest**

Some common signs of interest include but are not limited to:

- A steady gaze of eyes towards the item or person in question
- Some squinting also might happen in the eyes as a person attempts to see the item or person in question better
- Eyebrows slightly raised
- Lips pressed tightly together
- Head straight or push slightly forward with neck elongating
- Lips in a soft or gentle smile

- **Common signals of boredom**

Some common signals of boredom within the face and the head may include but are not limited to:

- Eyes looking away from the object or individual in question;
- Face generally unmoving but relaxed;
- Corners of the mouth turned downwards, or the lips pulled to the side; and
- Head being held up with a hand or supported in some other fashion.

- **Common signals of relief**

Some common signals of relief within the face and head include but are not limited to:

- Eyebrows their tilted outwards or lowered on the outer edges and higher on the inner edges;
- A mouth that is either slightly open or smiling; and
- A head tilted upwards in surprise.

- Common signs of surprise

Some common signs of surprised within the face and head include but are not limited to:

  - Eyes wide pupils dilated;
  - Eyebrows push high on to the head with extreme wrinkling of the forehead;
  - Mouth open with a lower chin; and
  - Head that is tilted back or tilted to the side.

- Common signs of disgust

Some common signs of disgust within the face and head include but are not limited to:

  - Head or eyes turned away from the object or person in question
  - Nostrils flaring or nose twitching
  - Nose crinkled or mouth snoring
  - Mouth closed
  - Tongue possibly sticking out
  - Chin that's jutting out away from the neck and body

- Common signs of shame

Some common signs of shame within the face and head include but are not limited to:

  - Head or eyes turn downwards looking at the ground;
  - Eyebrows low on the face but not forcefully so; and
  - The skin may be bright red or flushed.

- Common signs of pity

Some common signs that somebody is feeling pity for another individual within the face and head include but are not limited to:

  - Staring off into the distance possibly with some dampness or moisture;
  - Eyebrows pulled together slightly in the middle or pulled downward at the edges;

- ◦ Mouth wood corners turning downward; and
- ◦ Add maybe tilted to the side or tilted forward ever so slightly.

- • Common signs of calmness

Some common signs that somebody is feeling very calm in an event or situation within the face and head include but are not limited to:

- ◦ Facial muscles that are relaxed;
- ◦ Steady gaze looking forward with the eyes; and
- ◦ The mouth may be turned up slightly at the sides in a soft smile.

How to Look Certain Ways

Within this section, we will discuss how to come off in certain ways to those around us. If you want to make someone believe that you are a certain type of individual, these are some of the things you will want to think about.

Trustworthiness

Psychologists and body language experts have agreed that many individuals find the most trustworthy face is one that appears to have a slight smile. These individuals will have the corners of their mouths turned upwards ever-so-slightly with eyebrows that are raised just barely on the face. You must remember that the eyebrows must not be pushed up forcefully with many wrinkles on the forehead. These features show an individual as looking confident and friendly but without being overbearing or afraid of others not similar to them.

Intelligence

Many scientists and body language experts have agreed that people with a narrower face and a thinner chin tend to be more intelligent than others. In addition to this, people also tend to view those with larger noses as a common stereotype of how intelligent a person can be. Contrastingly, an individual with an oval face and a large chin is often stereotyped as having lower intelligence levels. Interestingly, it has also been shown that people tend to perceive others as having a higher intelligence when an individual is smiling or showing happiness, while people tend to judge others as having lower intelligence when they're showing signs of anger or sadness. You can artificially appear to be more intelligent by using certain signs of power body language. Signs of power body language include things such as speaking expressively, using a lot of eye contact, acting confident, and being modest in your clothing choices.

The Chin

The chin is a dominant and obvious corner of the face. All corners of the face have their own clear body language symbols that are unique to them. This is because a corner on your face is an area where its different parts converge and, as such, is the beginning and end of certain facial expressions. Within this section, we will explain the intended or unintentional meanings behind certain movements of the chin.

• Protection - the chin is a very vulnerable point on the face, as it tends to jut out and become easy to attack with one's fists. The chin lies just above the throat, which is an even more vulnerable spot. The chin can often act as a protector of the throat in cases of extreme vulnerability. There, they may be feeling defensive for some reason. Holding in the chin also tends to lower one's head, which then tends to be a submissive gesture. This is different from the defensive move we discussed earlier because the head is tilted down and because the eyes are often staring at the ground. This can be considered as a shy or flirtatious motion.

• Jutting - the chin can serve as a subtle method of pointing at other things. Flicking the chin or tilting the head may give a slight signal that only individuals in the know are going to notice. Jutting chin outwards towards a person is exposing it and sort of sending a message that they are daring a person to attack them. This is often considered a signal from defiance. Men with larger chins are often considered to have more testosterone than others. Because of this, the action of a man with a very large chin cutting it out enhances this idea by giving a mental symbol to those around them that they are *alpha*. It is often the case that if a person is feeling more confident than normal, their chin will stick out ever-so-slightly because they are holding their head up or are maybe tilting their head back a little bit. Pushing the chin outwards also tends to expose the teeth, and that can be considered as a threat because subconsciously, they may want to bite another person.

- Touching - when an individual is seen stroking their chin, it is often taken as a signal that the person is thinking very long and hard. They may be judging or evaluating a person or a situation. If a conversation has offered them a choice or decision to make, they may do this action to show that they're thinking it over. The head is one of the heaviest parts of our body and is held up exclusively by the neck and the spine. This can cause a lot of exhaustion and tenseness, and as a result, people are often seen cupping their head in their hand. This may be a sign of boredom or sleepiness. A more complicated symbol shown by holding the chin is to prevent the head from moving. This can show that the individual in question subconsciously wants to send a particular head signal but does not want to send the signal at the same time because of some kind of logical reasoning.

- Beard - beards have a very interesting connotation in terms of body language. In our society, clean-shaven tends to be the more widely accepted form of facial hair. Hence, within modern society, a beard is sometimes considered a sign that an individual is a non-conformist. A person with a full and luscious beard is more likely to be thought of as someone with no vanity needs and is usually considered confident and relaxed. On the other hand, when a beard is shaped and kept very neatly trimmed, it may show that a person is vainer and fussier than a normal individual. If a beard is seen as being unkempt or grows very wildly around an individual space, people may take this as a sign that the said guy is untidy or tends to be sloppy. The action of one stroking a beard can be seen as a preening gesture. This gesture symbolically makes one appear more beautiful and sends a signal that they believe themselves to be more attractive than the average person.

- Puckered - a chin that is seen as being puckered or pulled in particular directions and appearing to be wrinkled can be seen as a defensive stance because it can be put under the general idea of pulling back one's chin.

The Mouth

The mouth is a very important aspect of our face. It has probably the most muscles of any other region of our face and, as such, is used to convey the most complex forms of body language as well as verbal language.

- Breathing - by design, humans are meant to breathe through their nose, but when in need of more than the usual oxygen, we may use our mouth to breathe in larger gusts of air. If an individual is suddenly beginning to breathe through their mouth at quite a fast pace almost to the point of panting, they may be seen as frightened or angry because they are subconsciously preparing for the flight-or-fight reaction. The breathing of a stressed person may include actions such as gulping in a large gust of air or blowing it out very fast. If a person is extremely and overwhelmingly stressed, they may begin to hyperventilate. When an individual does yawn, it is often taken as a sign that a person is tired or bored. If an individual gives a short or deep exhaling sigh, they can be viewed as showing sadness or frustration. Inhaling air in a short and quick fashion—especially inconsistent sequences—can be viewed as silence sobs, and that is an indicator that a person is feeling deep and suppress sadness.

- Speaking - a mouth tends to send even more signals while they're speaking than through the traditional verbal language. If a mouth is moving very little and includes mumbling, this may be a sign that an individual does not feel like speaking, which could have possibly stemmed from shyness or from a fear that they will reveal too much about something. Moving very rapidly and a lot—at the same time that someone is speaking—can indicate that they are feeling extreme levels of excitement or dominance. People who speak very quickly tend to be visual thinkers who are trying to say what they see as quickly as possible. An individual who speaks very slowly may be considered a deep thinker and maybe trying to be careful about finding the correct words.

- Eating - the way that individuals eat can tell a lot of things about their personality. A person that views manners and very high regards will open their mouth as little as possible to put a tiny amount of food in and will keep it closed while they carefully chew. These individuals will never speak when they have food in their mouth. Opposite to this, a person who does not view manners in very high regard will push large mouthfuls into their wide mouth and will tend to chew and talk at the same time. Interestingly, there are some individuals who turn these tendencies onto their heads by eating very noisily as a sign that they are enjoying the food. These people are very snobbish about their food choices.

- Covering – sometimes, individuals use their hands to cover up their mouth. In modern society, exposing the inner parts of your mouth may be considered rude in some circles—hence, the hand is used to cover the mouth when yawning or laughing hard.

- Smiling - smiling has a very interesting depth to which it conveys emotion. Many individuals will look at a smile and simply think that is conveying the fact that someone is happy—when in reality, a smile can mean many different things, depending on context. A full smile is one that uses the entire face—this sort of smile will include the eyes and cheeks as well as the eyebrows. The eyes will crease, the eyebrows will raise, and the cheeks will lift up words. If an individual is smiling only with their lips, they are often trying to trick another individual. These smiles are typically fake that are not to be trusted. A genuine smile, on the other hand, tends to be asymmetric and is usually much larger on one side of the face. If an individual has a lopsided smile, then they're most likely a trustworthy person. However, if an individual does smile with their lips pushed tightly together, they may be showing signs of embarrassment. If an individual is smiling only half of their mouth on one side of their face, they may be showing sarcasm or uncertainty.

- Laughing - there are many different types of laughs in this world. Each one has its own meanings and signals in the realm of body language. Laughing can sometimes act as a sort of bonding mechanism between men and women. It is a well-known fact that women tend to laugh towards men that they like, while men enjoy it when women laugh at them. A woman laughing at a man is said to be a sign that she likes him. Laughing can also be used as a way of sending signals that one views another in terms of friendship. Laughing at jokes is often a requirement if you are friends with the person giving the joke. Laughing or smiling at the misfortune of those around us is often considered unacceptable within our society. As we are humans, we often can't help but find certain misfortunate events funny. Because of this, you may see suppressed laughter or people trying very hard not to smile as somebody experiences one of these unfortunate events.

- Biting or sucking - an individual that is sucking on their finger is often a recollection of actions of our childhood, as we tend to suck on our thumbs when we were children. Young children will suck on their fingers as a substitute for the breast. Because of this, this action is considered as a comforting one. This may be a sign that a person is feeling uncomfortable or stressed in a particular situation and that they are simply trying to comfort themselves through sucking on fingers, which then brings them back to that comforting feeling of having a breast in their mouth when they were an infant. Variance on this includes actions such as sucking or biting on the knuckles, the side of the hands, or other parts of the body. Sometimes, this may include the lips or inner cheek. Sometimes, this includes an outside object such as a pen or a pencil. All of these indicate a sign of stress or discomfort.

The Nose

Within this section, we will go through common signals sent out by the nose. Because the nose is stationed right in the middle of the face, it can send a large number of body symbols.

- Flare - when the nostrils have been widened and flared, it allows more oxygen to be breathed in by an individual. Subconsciously, this is an act of making a person ready for combat. Because of this, this can indicate that an individual is experiencing extreme displeasure or maybe feeling threatened.

- Wrinkle - if a nose is being wrinkled, it may be a sign that a person senses a bad smell from a certain area. It can also be a metaphor for the coming of something bad. An example of this is when an individual suggests something that another person dislikes, they may wrinkle their nose at that idea. Another variation of this idea is if a person is thinking about something or having certain ideas but are not satisfied with those ideas or thoughts.

- Touching – when an individual is touching their nose, it may be a sign that a person detects a terrible smell. It can also come across as a common signal from a person who's lying. Touching the nose indicates that somebody is lying when combined with the right combination of other bodily symbols. If a person flicks, then know that this may be a sign that they disagree with something a previous individual has said. If an individual is pinching the bridge of their nose, they may be thinking very hard about something. Usually, this is combined with some kind of frustration, as a person may be having difficulty making up their mind. Placing a finger on the nose or pressing it down is sometimes a habit or natural tick that a person has when they are thinking very deeply about something.

The Eyes

- Looking up – when an individual is seen to be looking upwards, they are often thinking very hard about a certain idea. When in the middle of giving a prepared speech or presentation, they may be attempting to remember their prepared words if they are looking up. Looking upwards and to the left may show signs that someone is attempting to recall a memory. Contrastingly, somebody who is looking upwards and to the right can show signs of imaginative construction, which then shows that they are making something up on the spot. Look it up can also be considered as a sign of boredom, as a person is trying to examine or understand their surroundings in order to find something better to do. If a person's head is lowered and if their eyes are looking at another person through their eyelashes, this may be considered a koi and suggestion of action, as it is used in combination with the idea of submission with the head down and the eye contact of attraction. However, when combined with a frown, this can be considered as a judgmental look.

- Looking down – looking down at a person can be considered an act of confidence, power, or domination. If a person is looking up at another person, then they may be showing a sign of submission. This may also be a sign that a person is feeling particularly guilty. If a person is looking downwards and to the left, this may be a sign that they are trying to talk to themselves without being noticed. However, if an individual is looking down and to the right, this may be a sign that they are dealing with certain internal emotions or internal turmoil at the moment. There are some cultures and societies in which direct eye contact is considered a rude or dominance symbol. Because of this, people in these societies may look down while talking to others in order to show respect.

- Looking sideways - the majority of our vision tends to be in the horizontal plane. Hence, if an individual seems to be looking sideways, that means that they are actively turning their head in order to see something they couldn't have already seen. A swift glance to the side is sometimes considered a symbol that somebody is just checking for the source of a distraction. This may also be considered a sign of irritation. If a person looks directly to the left, this can indicate that a person is trying to recall a sound in their memory. On the flip side, looking to the right can show that a person imagines a sound. If a person's eyes are moving from side to side rapidly, this may be a sign that a person is not to be trusted or that they are lying. This goes back to the idea that an individual is looking for an escape route in case they are found out or attacked.
- Gazing - the act of gazing is a sign that somebody is very interested in figuring out whatever they're looking at by staring at something with the intent of trying to understand it at a deeper level. This may be a sign that an individual is very interested in another. If, after locking eyes with another individual, a person continues to look into that person's eyes, then it may be a sign of love. If the eyes slide down over the individual's body, it is more likely to be a sign of lust. The place where one's eyes go is important. Gazing at an individual's mouth can indicate that a person would like to kiss them. Looking at individual sexual regions tends to show a desire to have intercourse with that person. Sliding the eyes up and down a whole person is usually considered an act of sizing an individual up. This may either be seen as a potential threat or as looking for a sexual partner, depending on where the eyes linger. This may be considered insulting in modern society.

As we can see from the contents of this chapter, the face and head of an individual's body contains some of the most expressive and potent forms of body language. Within this chapter, we have gone through the meanings of various different forms of body language that exclusively include the head and face connection. It is important to remember that when you are trying to analyze the actions of a person's head or face, you must take into account all parts and all corners of that person's face. You cannot judge a person's emotions simply through one action of one part of their face. You must take in their face as a whole and consider all of the possible meanings to all the different parts. For this chapter, we have gone through and analyze the different expressions and meanings behind certain movements of the eyes, smiles, lips, and many more. Within the next chapter, we will begin to explain how you can tell if there's truth in your relationships.

The Forehead

The forehead is often ignored in the realm of body language. This is a huge mistake, as the forehead is often a starting point for a wider set of body language signals. It is just above the eyes and, as such, can be looked at without sending different signals. Many people, when wanting to avoid people reading their forehead signals, will wear a large hat and keep their head down. This is particularly common in gamblers.

- Wrinkling - if a forehead is wrinkled, it is often due to the movement of an individual's eyebrows. Because of this, the wrinkling of the forehead acts as an amplifier of the eyebrow signals. This may indicate surprise or questioning.

- Sweating - as humans, we often excrete sweat on our heads first as compared to the other parts of our bodies. Sweating upon the forehead not only occurs when we are hot due to external temperature but also when we are hot due to internal energy and arousal. It is important to remember that an individual can also experience what is known as a cold sweat, which then indicates great amounts of fear and may be accompanied by moisture in the eyes.

- Touching - rubbing of the forehead is often considered a form of body language that signifies a greeting. Slowly rubbing the forehead can tend to indicate deep thinking or deep contemplation. If an individual is viewed rubbing their temples on either side, this can be a sign of stress or an incoming headache.

Chapter Seven: Truth and Relationships

Relationships are filled to the brim with extremely potent signs of body language. Which among the signs are positive or negative depends on the relationship. Unfortunately, relationships are also often full of lying amongst the couple. To help you understand your own relationship and the relationships of others, within this chapter, we will be going through how you can tell if somebody is lying in a relationship. We will also go through how you can analyze relationships that you are not in and how to tell if the individuals within that relationship have a good and positive connection with one another. You will also learn how to judge if the individuals in a relationship truly love their respective partners. You will also learn how to tell if somebody loves you truly and wholly. You will also learn some common signs when a female is ready for dating or wants to date an individual. You will also then learn its counterpart signs for men. This chapter will be very beneficial to anyone thinking about being in a relationship or is currently in a long-term relationship.

Lying

Being able to tell if somebody is lying to another person is a very important and powerful skill. Within a relationship lying, is unfortunately very common and very often seen in modern-day society. Being able to tell when an individual is lying may save you from painful and possibly emotionally damaging relationships. It is easier to detect if someone is lying when you are outside of the relationship, but you can also use these tactics when you are inside it as well. The following are a few signs that a person is lying to their significant other:

- A common scientific sign that somebody's lying is seen within the nose. Specific tissues within the nose are known to get engorged or to swell up when an individual is lying. Because of the swelling, a person's cells within their nose tend to release histamine, which will make the nose feel itchy. Because of this, an individual may be seen scratching or touching their nose. This indicator is not a tell-all-be-all of somebody lying. You need to take the sign in contact with many other symbols of lying.
- Another big sign that somebody is lying is a tendency to cover or block their mouth or to cover or rub their eyes. This is often done subconsciously, in hopes that a person would not be able to see those parts of their face and that they wouldn't be

able to tell that they are lying. They may also turn their head or body away when making crucial statements that, if seen past, will definitively suggest that they are lying.

- An individual may be known to overbearingly refer to certain religious phrases in order to make their lie sound more plausible. These are phrases such as: "I swear on my mother's grave" or "God, no." By adding religion or the afterlife into a statement, a person increases the weight of that statement and, as such, makes the other individual think that they are sincere.
- Phrases of denial such as "trust me," "honestly," "and to be perfectly honest" are attempts at being evasive and trying to avoid the original subject matter. If a person is attempting to change the perception of others about their actions, they may use these different evasive techniques. If these phrases are being repeated in excess and are popping up over and over, they may be clues that a person is lying.
- Individual appearing to be overly defensive or to overreact at certain situations that seem completely random to you may be a sign that they are lying. An example of this would be if an individual you're in a romantic relationship with gets off the phone—and when you ask who they were talking to, they'd respond with some type of hostile statement such as "Why are you so nosey?" A response such as this is completely uncalled for and indicates that a person is feeling guilty about a certain situation. For this instance, this individual is also appearing to try to place their feelings of guilt and mistrust onto the other person. This is an instant sign that a person is lying to you.
- If an individual has a well-known and long-winded history of lying, then they are more likely to be lying to you. People often continue to do what they know well, and if a person knows how to live very well, it is very likely that they will lie to you.
- If a person makes an exaggerated or extreme amount of eye contact, they may be lying to you. The common misconception is that people will avoid eye contact upon being embarrassed or ashamed. Because so many people know about this fact, people who are trying to keep something from you will actually do the opposite. They will go out of their way and try to make eye contact with you under any means necessary. This is an attempt to make themselves appear sincerer than they actually are. It is important to cautiously approach an individual who normally doesn't give much eye contact and then suddenly does a lot now.
- A person will often touch their face when they are lying. This is an attempt to put something in between them and the person they're lying to. This subconsciously

makes it easier to lie to a person because they feel as though they are not directly doing it.

- An individual trying to make a lie seem very believable and sincere may give a fake smile to a person. A way of being able to tell if somebody is lying through a fake smile is by looking for a smile that happens around the mouth but does not meet the eyes. This means that their cheeks or eyes may be without wrinkles or maybe particularly relax. This is a sign they are trying to force something.

- If an individual's pupils are dilating while they are speaking, this is a sign that they are feeling a very strong emotion. If combined with other telltale signs of lying, this may be a sign that an individual is lying to you. You have to be careful with this sort of signal because pupils may dilate for a number of different reasons. Typically, eyes will dilate for any sort of strong or overwhelming emotion. Because of this, an overwhelming feeling of shame or embarrassment will make a person's eyes dilate. As said, if combined with other signs of lying, this may, indeed, be an indicator that a person is lying. If not, this may simply be an indication that a person feels very strongly about you.

- Saying the word "honestly" too often in a conversation can be an indicator that somebody is lying. By saying the word "honest" over and over again, a person is subconsciously trying to convince you that they are honest. Because of how hard they are trying to do this, they may overcompensate and say it too many times to be believable.

- If you would like to be able to detect a liar very quickly, a good place to start is by asking very neutral questions. By asking a basic or non-threatening question, you will be able to observe a baseline response for the person telling the truth carefully. Asking them about things like the weather, their plans, or anything that would elicit a comfortable, easy response will give you a baseline understanding of what their body language is when they're telling the truth. You should continue this until you find a series of patterns that match their continuous truth-telling tendencies.

- The next step in trying to detect a liar very quickly is to move into emotionally charged questions. During this time, you should observe the presence or absence of changes in body language, facial expressions, eye movements, and even the way that they formulate their sentences. If any of this is inconsistent with the previous information that you gathered, by asking merely the easy questions, you may be looking at a liar.

- When trying to indicate or evaluate a liar, it is important to listen very closely to the tone, cadence, and even the sentence structures of the person speaking to you. A person who is lying may slightly change the tone or speed of their speech. They will do this subconsciously. A person trying to speak more quickly when lying will be doing so to try and get the lies out of them and get it over with as quickly as possible. A person speaking in a slower tone may be doing so because they are trying to think about what they're going to say next and are overly conscious about the movements of their body.
- A person that is lying will often start to remove themselves from their tale when answering your questions. They will try to direct the focus on to the people around them. You will begin to hear fewer I's and me's as they try to distance themselves from the lie that they are telling subconsciously.

Ways to Analyze the Truthfulness of a Relationship

It is very difficult to analyze a relationship when you *are* in one. Because of this, the following section will be speaking exclusively about relationships that you are the outsider of. This section of this text will explain how to analyze a relationship for truthfulness. This will cover both the man and the woman. Within this section, you will learn how to tell and analyze if there are inconsistencies within their relationship such as infertility and cheating. We will begin with a few questions that are crucial to making this analysis possible.

1. Is there trust? Trust is a crucial part of every relationship. In order to properly analyze your relationship, you have to know whether or not there is trust within it. How to tell if there's trust in a relationship is by examining it and seeing if the individuals within are able to be apart from one another easily and comfortably without any worries. They may miss each other but not to the point that they are constantly asking each other what they are doing. They do not feel happier when they're away from their partner, but they also do not feel insecure for the same reason. Insecurities are key here. A person that is in a loving and healthy relationship will not

feel insecure simply because of their significant other is not with them. If a person feels insecure every single time that they are away from their partner, this may be a sign that they do not trust that individual to make good decisions on their own.

2. Are they on the same page? Obviously, in good relationships, you do not always have to agree. However, it is important to have similar goals and similar views of the future. If a pair of individuals have very different ideas of their future and very different views for their lives, it may cause problems within a relationship down the road. It is very difficult to continue a long-term relationship with somebody who wants a very different future from another person.

3. Do they have respect for one another? Respect is very important in a relationship. Respect can be defined as being fond of the essence of a person without wanting to change them. An individual who respects their partner will be willing to put aside any kind of issues that a person has or any little quirks or flaws that are a part of their personality. In fact, it is best in a relationship when a person finds these flaws or quirks to be beautiful. However, if an individual puts down their significant other because of their flaws are quirks, this is a sign that they are not truly in love with them.

4. Can they speak openly with one another? Good, positive communication is an absolute must-have for a good relationship. If a couple that is together cannot have good communication with each other, it is very likely that they will not last very long. Good communication is when two individuals are able to speak about anything and everything that is on their minds, and they will not be shut down or told to stop speaking. The other person will listen intently and will give their side as well. There should be no boundaries on what these two can speak about with each other.

5. Are they equals? Equality is very important in modern-day relationships. Putting the same amount of work into a relationship is very important. If the work within the relationship is equally distributed amongst the two people, then they will have a much happier relationship. However, if one person is carrying the relationship or if the other person is leaning very heavily on the former's actions, they will begin to feel bogged down and will eventually feel as though their significant other is more of a chore than a relationship. Never should a person in a relationship feel as though they have to do something for their partner just because their partner wants them to. However, they should want to do something nice for their partner because they love them. If they begin to feel resentful for the things that they do for their partner, that might be a sign that they should end the relationship soon.

6. Do they enjoy being together? This one is fairly simple and obvious to understand. People in a relationship together should be able to enjoy and appreciate the simple things. You should want to be around your partner—it should feel somewhat "empty" if your partner is away from you, and it should feel happy just because you are around them.

7. Are they comfortable being themselves? This one is very important in a relationship. If a person is uncomfortable in their own relationship, then it is not likely to last very long. A person should not mind showing their weaknesses to their partner. Their partner should also be very supportive of that person's weaknesses and vice-versa. Another way to tell that there is comfort in a relationship is that if things are not going right for a certain person, they should go to their partner for comforting. If an individual is feeling anxious or self-conscious around their significant other, then it might be a sign to end the relationship soon. Individuals in a very good relationship with one another and are very comfortable with each other's company will usually understand their partner without having to speak a word.

8. Do they bring out the best in each other? Individuals that are in a good relationship with each another should be able to complement their partner very well. Being with another person should make you strive to be a better person and should not make you feel bogged down as though you are being pulled in a worse direction by being with them.

By beginning with these questions, you should be able to analyze a relationship from the outside carefully. Keep in mind that those that are in a relationship will know the background of their connection the best. Hence, begin with these questions when trying to analyze another relationship, but always take into account the understanding of those within it.

How to Tell If Love Is Truly There

Using the analysis questions that we previously discussed, we can begin to figure out and understand if love is truly present in a relationship. This is obviously very important for long-lasting and comfortable relationships. If love is not actually present and if the individuals in the relationship are mistaking lust for love, there can be serious problems. With this being said, love is sometimes difficult to understand and to pinpoint. That's why within this section, we will go through some easy ways to tell if there really is love present in a relationship.

1. When the individuals within a relationship want to spend time with each other and want to spend the majority of their day spending quality time with the other person, this is probably an indicator of true love. This desire and need to spend time with each other are a sign of successful long-term intimacy. If the individuals in question truly care about each other, they will make time to spend with one another in between all of their daily commitments.

2. Individuals that are truly in love with one another in a relationship will ask about the other person's day. This may seem like a very simplistic and easy way to tell if there is true love in a relationship—*and it is*. This is because by asking about a person's day, you are showing interest in that person's life. This is a very important sign of love. If an individual does not care enough to ask a person about their day, then they do not care about the inner workings of that person's life and are not truly in love with them.

3. Trust is very important in good and strong relationship partners who truly and deeply care about each other and will give the other person in their relationship the benefit of the doubt. Research has shown in the past that the majority of successful and long-term relationships have one thing in common—that is a deep and powerful trust between the individuals involved. If individuals feel as though the other person in the relationship does not trust them, it will make them not want to trust them in turn. This level of distrust within a relationship will destroy it very quickly. If a person feels as though they're not being trusted and are being questioned at every turn, they may feel trapped in a relationship and may want to end it very quickly.

4. Individuals in a relationship in which they care very deeply for and truly love each other will be more than willing to offer help when the other person needs it. Oftentimes, an individual will not have to ask for this help, as the other person will simply offer it up in the first place. This is a very beautiful and strong sign of love. This is because a person who offers help when somebody needs it is clearly paying attention to the needs of that person and wants that individual to be happy and healthy at all times. Because of these wants and needs, that person will offer to help them despite the inconveniences that they put upon themselves.

5. Individuals in a relationship do not necessarily always have to agree on everything,

but they should show respect for the other person's views. Strong love in a relationship can show itself—and individuals that, while they disagree, will also be respectful and not put down the ideas or beliefs of the other person.

6. Individuals that feel very strong and good love for one another will include the other person in their decision-making. Good strong couples will decide on everything from the mundane to the extremely important things together. This is because they will want to include the other person in their everyday life.

7. The next indicator of true love in a relationship seems fairly obvious. A couple that shows clear and obvious affection for one another are typically very emotionally intimate and in love with each other. This is not always having to translate through sex. Emotional intimacy can show itself through very simple signs like standing closely together or softly touching another person. These touches indicate a strong feeling of connection between the two individuals. They also show through these signals that they want to be physically closer to the other person at all times no matter where they are during the day.

Female Dating Signs

Within the next section, we will go through some common signs that a female is ready to date or is interested in another person.

1. The first sign that a female is interested in dating another person is how often or seldom that person touches you. These are not often strong touches or full-on hugs or kisses, but a female that is looking to date an individual finds excuses to touch them in subtle ways. They might brush against the other person, they might throw a teasing punch at the other person's shoulder, or they might even move closer towards the other person in the middle of a conversation. If a female is not actively trying to touch another person in subtle ways, that may be a sign that she is not interested or not open to dating at the moment.

2. Another sign that a female is interested in dating another person is their ability to maintain eye contact. A woman attempting to catch another person's eye from across the room or looking very intently into another person's eye while they are speaking is a sure-fire sign that they are least interested in you as a friend. You are able to tell whether or not she's interested in the other person as more than just a

friend upon combining these signs with the others that we will be discussing. In general, though, maintaining strong and good eye contact is a good sign that a female is interested in what the other person is saying and that they hold their opinion to high regard.

3.   Another sign that a female is interested in dating another person is how often they ask personal questions. A female that wants to date an individual will try to learn as much about them as she possibly can. This may lead to her asking deep or probing questions, and the other individual may find themselves in a deep conversation about the universe without even realizing it. This is a sign that she's very interested in that person's opinions.

4.   A female that is willing to laugh with an individual is a sure-fire sign that they at least find them attractive. A woman laughing with another person means that she is having a good time with them and enjoy spending time with them. Women love men who can make them laugh—especially if the jokes that a person is giving off are not actually *that* funny, in case that a person is still laughing at them, it is a very good sign that she is interested in that person.

5.   Another sure-fire sign that a woman is very interested in another person is if she's obviously mirroring the other person's body language. An individual who is interested will the consciously marry their body language in an attempt to make them like each other even better. This is because instinctively, as people, we tend to like people better that look like us—and by mirroring our body language, we can artificially make the other person believe that we look like them and make them like us better without them even realizing it. If a female is doing this continuously to another person, this is a very good sign that she is interested in dating them.

6.   A very common action of flirting that a woman participates in when she's interested in dating another person is teasing. Women will often tease men that they would like to go out with or that they want the attention of.

7.   A woman who replies very swiftly to another person is often interested in that person. Quick responses from a woman is a very good sign that she's interested in dating the other person.

8.   Another very good sign that a woman is interested in dating another person is when she's willing to make plans immediately at the end of a date. If she is setting up another date, it almost certainly means that she's interested in continuing to engage in romantic encounters with them. If she doesn't want to be that obvious, then she might say things that hint towards her wanting to set up another date. This might

include her giving days that she's free or saying that it would be nice to meet up again. This is a very obvious and clear sign that a woman wants to continue dating.

9. Another very good sign that a woman is interested in dating another person is if she tends to remember the things that the said person says. Without even realizing it, women tend to memorize things better when they're interested in them. This is because they hold a high level of importance on the things that they are interested in. Hence, if you find that a woman is remembering every little thing that you are saying to them later on, then this is a very good sign that she's interested in dating you. Women who are interested in other people will show their interest by remembering the small details of every conversation.

10. Another great sign that a female is interested in dating another person is if they are willing to give a very high level of detail about their past relationships. If a female has a very complicated or difficult past with relationships and is willing to let her new partner know about it, then it is a very good sign that she wants to have a strong relationship with this person. By opening up and giving her deepest vulnerabilities and showing the other person her past, she's telling them that she trusts them and believes that they will not treat her the way that some of her previous partners did.

11. Another very good sign is that the female is not afraid to let the other person know when she is having doubts or having difficulty in a relationship. This is a sign of very good and strong communication within a relationship and implies that she's interested in keeping the dating or relationship going for as long as she possibly can. If a female who wants to continue dating a person is having difficulty in a relationship, she will try to fix it by bringing it out into the open and letting everyone know about what's going on and trying to fix it.

12. Another huge sign that a female is very interested in dating another person is if she is willing to invite that person to a family function. This is a very big deal, especially if that female has a very good and strong connection with her family. Introducing a new person to a family that she is very close to and have strong ties with is a sign that she is feeling comfortable enough around that person to introduce that person to her family.

Male Dating Signs

Within the next section, we will discuss and go over some common signs that a man wants to date another person.

1. If a man appears to want to spend a lot of time with a person and to make a special effort to be around them, then this is a very good sign that they want to date that person. This shows that a man is actively creating time to be with another person and shows that they are committed to being with that person. This is a sign that a person is willing to put in an effort to be around that person and thus would like a deeper and longer relationship.
2. A man that seriously wants to date an individual will want to do so in person and not through a computer or phone. An individual that wants a date or wants to "connect" through a computer is most likely not seriously interested in keeping a relationship with that person.
3. A man that is very interested in dating another person will be willing to court that person. In other words, they will want to make the first move because they care enough about the other person to put themselves out there.
4. A man that very much wants to continue a relationship and continue to date an individual will align their plans with that person. They will be careful to make sure that their plans are lined up with the other person's so that he can accommodate that other individual. This is a very good sign that a man wants to continue to date a person because it shows that he cares about them.
5. If a man is interested in dressing up and looking nice for another individual, this is a very good sign that he's interested in having a long-lasting relationship with that person.
6. If a man wants to ask about an individual's family and genuinely wants to meet them, he most likely wants to continue dating this person. Being interested in another individual's family background is a very good sign that a man wants a long-lasting and serious relationship with them. A man who's interested in a person's family and who likes their family clearly wants a long relationship with them.
7. If a man wants to introduce a person to everyone in his life, it is a sign that he is proud of that person and loves them very deeply.
8. Subtle protectiveness is another very good sign that a man wants to date another person. The key word here is "subtle." You do not want a man who is overly protective and doesn't want their partner (or prospective partner) to have their own life or friends, but some signs of protectiveness are good. If a man is gently protective of another person in ways that make them *genuinely* feel safe, it is a very

good sign that he wants to date them further.

9. Another very important sign that a man is interested in long-term dating a person is if he is very interested in and willing to have long meaningful conversations with that other person. This shows signs that he wants to know everything about them and is very interested in their background and their beliefs. This is a surefire sign that a man is interested in dating them.

10. A very good sign that a man is interested in a person as a long-term partner rather than just a one-time hookup is if he doesn't talk about that person's body very often. If he does talk about their body, it is in short and simple ways and doesn't usually include any type of derogatory terms. Typically, a man that is interested in a long-term relationship with another person will compliment them on their intellect or personality because subconsciously, he knows that those are things that will last a lifetime, while a person's body is only here for now.

11. Men are very forthcoming with their wants and needs. Hence, oftentimes, a man who's interested in continuing to date a woman will simply outright say it. Obviously, if a person receives a statement from a man saying that they want to date them continuously, this is a very good sign. Alternatively, if a person is constantly questioning and trying to figure out where they stand with a man and if that man is never giving straight answers, it is a very good sign that he does not want to date that person.

12. If a man does not go on very often about another woman, it is a very good sign that he is committed to that one person exclusively.

13. Hearing the phrase "I miss you" before you hear the phrase "I love you" is a very good sign that a man is interested in dating a person long-term. By indicating that he missed that person, you are showing that he's interested in being around them for a long time and in more than just a hookup. Saying "I miss you" to someone means a lot more than saying "I love you" in the first few stages of a relationship.

14. If a man's eyes tend to linger on yours rather than your entire body, this is a very good sign that he is interested in a long-term and serious relationship. This is because the eye contact of a man shows extreme interest in the person that he is looking at—and by not exclusively or deliberately staring at that person's body, he is showing that he genuinely cares more about that person's thoughts and beliefs than he does about their body.

Chapter Eight: Confidence and How It Is Displayed

Confidence is a very powerful emotion in today's society. An individual who appears very confident is able to go very far places. By appearing confident, a person can attract suitable mates as well as be given promotions based on their perceived leadership skills. Because of this, confidence is very commonly displayed in different ways. However, confidence is also faked a lot of times in order to get ahead in life. Within this chapter, we will go through the common ways that confidence is displayed through body language. In addition, we will also go through how you can spot a lack of confidence in an individual.

Displaying Confidence

- Posture

Posture is very important in the appearance of confidence. An individual's posture can say a lot about their perceived level of confidence. Confident posture is defined by legs that are lined with the individual's shoulders and feet approximately four to six inches apart. Weight is typically distributed equally on both legs, and shoulders are pushed back slightly. A straight back is also very typical of someone with extreme confidence. Individuals with this sort of posture are considered assertive and tend to project confidence. This is because an individual with this posture is seen as being able to "stand tall" regardless of their height and are also perceived as being very open to those that are talking to them, as they are unafraid of any attacks or criticism.

- Hands

Hands are very important in trying to appear confident. It is important to remember when trying to display confidence through your hands to keep them calm and still. Rapidly moving one's hands is a sign of nervousness or anxiety.

- Eye Contact

Having the ability to maintain long and strong eye contact with another is a very good sign that an individual is feeling confident. This is because showing eye contact with another person is a very vulnerable feeling and position. This is because our eyes can show a lot about how we actually feel in a situation. By maintaining good eye contact, we are showing to the other person that we are unafraid of what they may see within our eyes. This is a sign of extreme confidence, as it shows that you are self-assured in your feelings and believes that you are unafraid of how a person will interpret what they see in your eyes.

- Mirroring Body Language

Mirroring the body language of those around us elicits a sort of understanding and seeks acceptance from those around us. This raises our confidence level as we humans strive to be liked by those around us. Because those around us will subconsciously begin to like us more by mirroring their body language, they will also be confident because of their positive view of us.

- Fidgeting

It is very important to remember not to fidget when you are trying to display levels of confidence. Fidgeting in any form—no matter what part of your body is doing the movement—shows signs of nervousness and anxiety. In addition to this, it can simply annoy those around us. People are often irritated by constant rhythmic tapping or brushing noises. This is something to keep in mind if you are an individual who likes to bounce their leg or tap their foot at simple moments.

Ways to Spot a Lack of Confidence in a Person

- A very common sign of lack of confidence in an individual is if they are constantly touching their phone while in social situations or while alone. If an individual finds themselves unable to sit still during a social situation in which they don't know very many people, this may be a sign that they lack confidence. Checking their phone is a sign that they feel uncomfortable in a social situation and are unable to connect with those around them.

- Another sign of a lack of confidence in an individual is a quick backing down during a disagreement to avoid arguing with another person. An individual with an extreme lack of confidence will not want to cause problems with a person that they disagree with. Because of this, they often negotiate their views in order to avoid conflict. This shows that a person lacks confidence because they are not assured in their own opinions and would rather back down than express themselves honestly.
- Another common sign of a lack of confidence in an individual is their inability to leave their homes without any sort of makeup or hairstyling. This is a very obvious sign of a lack of confidence because it shows that an individual doesn't feel that they are worth being looked at unless they have something on their bodies or face to make them look more beautiful. Putting makeup on or doing their hair gives a false sense of self-esteem to an individual, which people with low self-esteem or confidence rely on very heavily.
- An individual with low confidence will also tend to take constructive criticism far too personally. If a person gives this individual constructive criticism about something, they will take it way too seriously and will end up feeling very strong negative emotions. This is a huge sign of low confidence and low self-esteem because this individual is not emotionally balanced enough to handle constructive criticism from those around them.
- Individuals who have low confidence or self-esteem will also find themselves afraid to contribute their opinion in a conversation. They will often second-guess themselves before they say anything instead of diving into an interesting conversation. They may find themselves stuttering or putting themselves down. This is because these individuals don't know how well their opinions will be received and are afraid of other people taking their opinions negatively. This is a sign of low confidence or self-esteem because these individuals care very deeply about how the people they make contact with view them.
- An individual who has difficulty with confidence also find themselves extremely indecisive with very simple and basic decisions. They may change their minds very often after coming to a decision. This is a sign of low self-confidence because this individual cannot trust their own opinions or decisions. This is especially a sign of low self-confidence when this applies to very simple tasks or simple decisions.
- Individuals with low self-confidence will also have extreme difficulty handling genuine compliments from those around them. They tend not to think that they are worthy of such good compliment, and they usually put them down or not accept them.

- Individuals struggling with low self-confidence will also tend to give up very soon with things that they are trying to do or achieve. They may have goals and dreams that they want to accomplish but will give up before they even really begin. This is a sign of low self-confidence because they do not believe that they have the ability to accomplish these goals and dreams before they even start.
- Individuals that struggle with low self-confidence will also tend to compare themselves with those around them. They tend to have very strong attention to the people that are doing better than them and will point out all of the ways that they are not doing as well as those around them. This is a strong sign of low self-confidence because it says that the person in question does not view themselves as very successful or doing very well in their life.
- Slouching is a very common display of low self-confidence in an individual. Why so? It is because lowering the center of a person's body is a sign that a person is not willing to hold up the weight of their upper body themselves. It sends off a signal that that individual is not proud of himself/herself. Because of these things, this is a big sign of low self-confidence.

In order to detect low self-confidence in an individual, all you have to do is look out for some of these common signs of low self-esteem and self-confidence. You can also detect low self-confidence or low self-esteem within yourself by looking out for these common signs. If you find that you or someone you know has low self-esteem or confidence, you can begin to work on them by saying very positive statements about yourself on a regular basis. Within the next chapter, we will go over how an individual can fix their body language and how they can pretend to be more confident than they really are.

Chapter Nine: How to Fake Your Body Language

Within this chapter, we will go through some easy and simple ways to fake your body language in order to come across as different emotions or expressions to those around you. These methods can be beneficial in everyday life as well as in the workplace. They can also serve you well in starting out relationships for the first time. These methods also do a good job of helping you feel how you are trying to feel. Have you ever heard the cliché, "Fake it till you make it?" Well, in some ways, this is true. By pretending to feel a lot of the emotions, you may be able to *convince yourself* that you actually feel that way.

1.   Taking a Deep Breath

By amplifying the supply of oxygen within our lungs, we can be given more power and more ability to fake our emotions through body language. This will also give us a moment to collect our composure and pretend to be calm and collected. In addition, deep breathing tends to stimulate the parasympathetic nervous system, which can trigger a relaxation response. This is very good, especially when trying to trick those around you into believing that you are calm and controlled in a situation. Deep breathing is a very good trick for mindful living, as it gives you more control over your body and your reactions to stimuli.

2. Controlling the Movement of Our Eyebrows

Our eyebrows can convey a lot about our inner feelings. A lot of movement from our eyebrows can convey feelings that you do not want to express. You need to consciously be aware of the movement of your eyebrows when you are trying to fake certain emotions through your body language.

3. Trying Not to Use a Fake Smile

While it is good to smile even if you don't feel like it, that is not always beneficial when faking your emotions through body language. While looking happy and bubbly may make others want to like you, it is not the best look to have constantly. Fake smiles are far too easy to see through, and humans are naturally inclined to try and search for any inconsistencies within somebody's smile. A better way to hide your emotions is to keep your mouth straight and not smiling or sad.

4.   Relaxing Your Face

By keeping your facial muscles relaxed, you can more easily control the movements of your face. Stay away from movements such as teeth grinding, frowning, or displaying any other type of emotional expression. Having relaxation and a calmer look on your face makes it more easy to control better the emotions you are putting out through your body language.

5.   Supporting Your Head

A person's head that is being held up by an individual or a face buried into one's palm is a very obvious and clear giveaway of a bad mood or sadness. It is better to keep your head held up high and your neck and back straight in a situation where you feel sad, but you do not want those around you to know that you feel sad. Another important thing to remember is to try and stop yourself from touching your face when you're feeling sad, as it is a strong sign of anxiety and stress.

6. Avoiding Fidgeting

Moving suddenly or very quickly are obvious signs of discomfort and anxiety. If you try to relax your body and try to look as though you are comfortable where you are, then it can be easier to control your emotions and feelings. It also becomes harder for those around you to decipher what you feel because you simply look calm and relaxed.

7. Speaking in a Balanced Tone

This one is very important. If you want to come across as anything other than how you are currently feeling, you may want to take a moment to think about what you're going to say and speak in a balanced and even tone to those around you. The tone of your voice can give away your thoughts faster than you could think. Speaking too fast or changing your tone very quickly and frequently is an obvious sign that you aren't quite sure what you are trying to emote or what you are feeling. Try to slow down before you answer any questions. In addition to this, try to speak with your mind in a logical setting. You will want to focus exclusively on facts and remove any emotion from the situation. Through focusing on facts, you can stop your body from exclusively feeling the said emotions and focus on the task at hand.

8. Trying to Disassociate

If you can manage to detach yourself from a situation you are in, it will become much easier to control your body language and the emotions that you were putting off. An easy way to do this is to think of happy thoughts as good memories. Doing this will help you take your mind off of whatever is happening around you, and it will make it more challenging for others to read your thoughts. By detaching yourself from the situation around you, you will more easily be able to see the logical side of what is happening and able to accurately portray the particular body language and emotions that you want to exude.

9.   Speaking to Yourself

You will be able to tell your mind to think about the way that it should. This will make it easier to control your body language and your emotions, as you are in the process of controlling your own mind.

Conclusion

Within this text, we have learned many important things about our own and other people's body language. In the very beginning of this text, I began by explaining why this book was written and why it is beneficial to the reader.

Within the first chapter, I began to go into how an average person can read those around them and explain how easy it is to read people and how it can be learned by just about anyone. I also began to give the basics of how to analyze the people around us, with a brief discussion on how important context is in reading people's words and actions, on how it is essential for us to take into consideration more than one point of observation when reading people and instead focus on how specific combinations of circumstances can more accurately represent how someone truly thinks and feels, on how to analyze someone you don't have a background of, as well as on how to ensure that your personal preference or judgment would not jeopardize your assessment of another person's emotions and motives.

Within the second chapter, I began to go into the way that our bodies talk our body language. I explained how there are gestures that evoke a positive impression on others in the same manner that there are ones that cause a negative impression as well. I explained how every part of the human body communicates in the feelings of a person. I also went through how body language can reveal our deepest inner emotions that we may not even recognize ourselves. I also began to go into some common gestures and what they mean in terms of body language. I then began to go into detail about nonverbal aspects that our bodies give off and what they may mean in different situations. I went into detail about the body language of the torso, hips, chest, shoulders, hands, fingers, legs, and feet. I also went to detail about how all of these things work together to create one full statement of body language.

In the third chapter, I began to go through the basic rules for analyzing those around us. Meanwhile, as for the fourth chapter, I discussed the difference between verbal and nonverbal communication. I explain how you can analyze the verbal statements that others make based on their nonverbal behavior. I also went into the intricacies of analyzing the nonverbal behavior that we may come into contact with on a daily basis.

Within the fifth chapter, I went into how our minds communicate with those around us. I went into detail defining the unconscious mind and the limbic brain and how they work together to create our personalities and emotions.

Within the sixth chapter, I went into the intricacies of reading the face and explained how you can use the face as a method of nonverbal communication and how you can read another person's facial expressions through the littlest of things. I explained how you could analyze every expressive portion of the face. I went into detail about analyzing and understanding the nonverbal communication with the eyes, smiles, expressions, lips, heads, and more.

Within the seventh chapter, I went into how you can tell if there is truth in a relationship. I went into detail about how you can tell if somebody is lying in a relationship and how to analyze a relationship between true love and honesty.

In the next couple of sections, I went into detail about the common signs that a female or a male is interested in dating somebody else. Meanwhile, in the eighth chapter, I went through how confidence is typically displayed in a person's body, how you can spot a lack of confidence in someone, as well as how you can fake some confidence in your own body.

Within the ninth chapter, I went into detail about some tips and tricks on how to fake your own body language. I went into detail about how you can learn to control your own emotions and your body language in order to give off different expressions and feelings to other people.

Within this text, I have successfully given a detailed guide on how to read those around us, as well as how to affect our own body language. All of the tips and tricks I have given within this text are greatly beneficial to the average person in terms of their social life as well as their workplace or school. I hope that you, as the reader, are able to find any use in all of the tricks in body language that I have given in this text. I also hope that you, the reader, are able to improve your current relationships and find yourself in higher economic standing because of this book.

Contents